Sean, Ezequiel, Dave
Ebook Contributors

Dear Newbie,

Congratulations on starting a difficult but exciting journey of learning about crypto. CoinYou will make the difficulty seem easy. This guide is a compilation of answers to frequently asked questions from every good FAQ we could find on the internet. We compiled and altered all of these public lists to create one master-guide.

CoinYou was started by Sean and Dave, two guys who wanted to make crypto easy for the people who can benefit from it the most: regular people. crypto knowledge shouldn't be hoarded by the top one percent.

The more you learn about crypto, the more you will realize how inevitable it is for this technology to become the future of money. It's already happening. This can seem scary at first, but once you learn the basics, its really empowering!

Learn more about the CoinYou.co mission to help the unbanked, refugees, minorities, and non-English speakers learn about crypto at CoinYou.Co/Mission.

Introduction

Congratulations if you are reading these words, it means that you are interested in one of the hottest topics in the world today. It doesn't matter if you are reading this because you found this document on the web intentionally or if someone called your attention to it for some reason. It's ok to be a little skeptical about its content. The important thing is that you're about to begin a journey that can enlighten you about how money works and how it can work much better for the benefit of many. In the current system, inequality and income disparity is a growing problem. Decentralizing technology like Bitcoin may hold the key to the equitable future we are all hoping for.

Your journey will make you think about many things that may be unknown to you at this point in your life. But this is okay. It is true that it may take a while until you're able to understand the system we will describe for you and its implications.

Don't worry. Everyone is a beginner at some point. We are a community of people that discovered how to use the internet to securely create and share value. This capacity is huge and it gives us the power to change things which must be changed. We'll try our best to help you learn the basic points of the revolution behind the technology and the market of Bitcoin and other cryptos. So let's move forward toward our goal.

Starting from Scratch.

We want people who know nothing about Bitcoin and Cryptocurrency to be able to learn the basics in one document.

You don't have to have a financial, cryptography or computer science background to understand the things we will share with you. Even if you don't understand something right away, get used to the topics and search for more info if you need to and you'll surely be compensated with wisdom.

Our e-book consists of a series of short questions and answers. We avoided technical discussions and concentrated on conceptual and practical things that relate to the most commons questions for newbies.

There is a glossary of terms at the end of the e-book. You can refer to it anytime you don't know a term in the text.

Financial Literacy

Knowing that the vast majority of the world's population is not educated on financial matters at a reasonable level, we will begin by briefly explaining some aspects of the current financial system that are key to the understanding of Bitcoin and Cryptos.

The paradigm of the financial system today is what we call "centralization". What it means in practice is that the important decisions that affects the whole system are made by only a few people and institutions. Centralization creates and concentrates enormous power, a power that is desired by people who want to lead the system in a direction to benefit themselves. All sorts of corruption, surveillance, and loss of data occur with centralization.

Decentralization is the key feature in Cryptos. Most Cryptos have no central authority, but work by strict rules defined and supervised by computer code. This can be a little complicated or mysterious to some of the readers, but this is how it works and our mission is to help you understand it step by step.

One more thing that you must know is that before Bitcoin and Cryptos existed, the centralized financial system was vulnerable to tyranny. Once a central authority is in place, it has power to control and change the rules whenever it wants to. This system is vulnerable to collapse. A study of the 2008 crash of the USA economy will show how close we came to collapsing the entire global financial system. In 2008, the US government bailed out the financial institutions that lead the economy to disaster. Many people were outraged because taxpayers paid for the banks risk and mistakes and no one was prosecuted for causing such a problem. One wonders if the next crisis can be averted.

Central bankers and governors print money to pay their bills and devalue everyone's money in doing so. Up until 2008, there was no way to escape this, and it was in this context that Bitcoin was born. Bitcoin came to light through the work of an anonymous creator called "Satoshi Nakamoto".

Satoshi delivered an **open-source** electronic cash system with no central authority. It is a purely **p2p** (peer-to-peer) system that is created and maintained by computers all over the world in a **distributed** way so that **consensus** is reached by mathematics. It's not dependent on any form of authority that can change anything in the system in a centralized way. Don't be afraid of any of these concepts. We will clarify them along the way for beginners to fully understand it. Bitcoin and Cryptocurrencies work in a very different way from the centralized banks that serve the central authorities of the countries of the world.

The main aspects of the crypto system is it's open nature (where anyone can transact without asking for permission) it's decentralized configuration (that enables strong networks without a single point of failure) and it's censorship resistance feature (that makes it nearly impossible to shut the system down).

In Bitcoin and other Cryptos, the **inflation** is mathematically predictable which ensures stability.

For these and others reasons, CoinYou is involved in getting people to know the basics of this technology, in the hope that they will securely participate in this revolution if they think it is worthwhile. Enjoy the journey!

What is Bitcoin?

This may be the simplest and most difficult question to answer in a short and understandable way for newbies. Bitcoin, to be short, is the first and most popular decentralized and peer-to-peer currency, created and stored electronically. It's not centrally controlled, nor are Bitcoins printed in the usual way that money is; instead, Bitcoins are made through software that solves mathematical problems.

Bitcoins belong to a growing category of digital money called cryptocurrency. One of Bitcoin's most distinguishing characteristics is that it's completely decentralized.
This means that it's network is not controlled by any one institution or government. This makes a lot of people feel secure because it means that a large bank or institution won't be able to control their money against their interest in any direction.

Who created Bitcoin?

The first Bitcoin paper was published in 2009 in a cryptography mailing list by someone calling themself Satoshi Nakamoto. Satoshi left the project in late 2010 without revealing anything. People do not know if Satoshi was an individual or a group of people, but the identity of the person(s) doesn't matter because the system is open source and it's run by code and not by "important people with central roles and authority", there is no such centralization in Bitcoin. The community has since grown exponentially with **many developers** working on Bitcoin.

Why was Bitcoin created?

Bitcoin's whitepaper was released in the context of the world's economy crash of 2008. The current financial system is based on debt and it's controlled centrally, these are the two main characteristics of the system's contrast with Bitcoin. Perhaps the creator wanted to offer an alternative financial system, based on computing and mathematical rules and with sound economic principles. Additionally, it is possible that Bitcoin was designed to be a safe haven for people to get out of the current financial system in times of financial trouble in the current system.

How can I get Bitcoin?

Use the following options to get Bitcoins:

- **Trading your services for Bitcoin** - You can earn bitcoins by offering services and good accepting bitcoin as payment for that. You can do almost any kind of jobs, specially those are done online, and receive your income in Bitcoin.

- **Selling Goods in Exchange for Bitcoin** – Similar to barter trade, you can actually exchange goods that you own for Bitcoin. It's another quick and convenient way of getting more of the digital currency.

- **Face to Face** – You also have the option of getting bitcoins in person. If you want anonymity or don't want to deal with banks, simply acquire Bitcoin via a face-to-face transaction with a local seller.

- **LocalBitcoins.com** – You can search for individuals selling Bitcoin in your area if you don't have any friend thats deals cryptos. It's easy. Simply enter the amount you wish to acquire, send the trade request and send your payment to the seller.

- **Online Exchanges and Wallets** – New to Bitcoin? There's a variety of exchanges and wallets that you can find, depending on your needs. Many exchanges and wallets will store amounts of digital and/or fiat currency for you – a lot like a regular bank account but a hardware wallet is the most secure way to store your crypto.

- **Bitcoin ATM** - you can withdraw or deposit bitcoins using Bitcoin ATM machines near you. There are not so many ATM options for everyone at this moment, but the number of options is on the rise.

- **Debit or Credit Card** - Some exchanges let you buy Bitcoin with a debit or credit card, such as CEX.io . Remember to consult your country options and limitations to this kind of service.

- **Other Cryptocurrencies** - You can buy bitcoins using other cryptocurrencies you might have. You can go to one of the many exchanges that offers this possibility.

- **Mining** - You can also be awarded bitcoins as a miner once you've verified transactions and they've been added to the public ledger, also known as the blockchain, you'll be given bitcoins for your service. Stay tuned in the fact that nowadays Bitcoin mining requires specific hardware and a high investment, so don't fall prey to those who promises you a "share" in bitcoin mining if you give them money. Make your research on every aspect of this kind of proposal and don't give money for anyone that cannot prove they own real mining machines and have a serious business model.

- **Affiliate Programs** - Some exchanges offers a kind of a bonus to raise the number of dealers in their platforms. They use to offer a small percentage of the transactions of persons you invite through a affiliate link to their platform, paid in Crypto directly to the profile of the owner of the affiliate links. This can be a good way to involve more people into Crypto and getting some coins for doing that.

- **Faucets** : Bitcoin faucets are websites that give small amounts of satoshis (how are called the small units of bitcoins) for people that perform some repetitive task during some time. In the past, there were a lot of faucets of Bitcoin, but now with the raise in price it's not so easy to find one that is trustworthy. One of the most well known is https://freebitco.in/ .

There are a lot of scams using faucets, so you must do a good search on the reputation of the website before investing your time and energy on that. Remember also that the reward for this is very shy and you can make more crypto in other ways.

How can I sell Bitcoin?

There are three main ways to sell Bitcoin:

• **Direct Trade** (p2p) — The first method involves a direct trade with another person, or using an intermediary to enable the transaction, such as LocalBitcoins.com.

• **Exchanges** — Use an online exchange to trade into their preferred currency, instead of another individual, to sell bitcoins.

• **Buying goods and services** — This method allows Bitcoin owners to sell their bitcoins for goods and services by sending them to individuals who wish to acquire cryptocurrency for their goods and services.

Why use Bitcoin?

There are many different reasons! People can use it for philosophical, political technological, economic or practical motivations. Whatever be the case, there are many advantages to using Bitcoin, which include:

• **Quick, Easy and Convenient** - You can send and receive bitcoins anywhere in the world at any time in a matter of a few minutes.

• **Low Fees** – Normally, the fees for Bitcoin transactions are very small when compared to other options. But it's good to know that Bitcoin fees can fluctuate due to the dynamic fee market. In addition, some wallets will also allow you to pay a fee you're willing to spend. With higher fees, you'll get faster confirmation of your transactions.

• **Secure** – When using Bitcoin, users remain in control of their transactions. You're also protected from identity theft since Bitcoin payments can be made without personal information associated with the transaction.

• **Transparent** - All information about Bitcoin transactions are fully available on the blockchain for anybody to verify and use in real-time.

How do Bitcoin Transactions Work?

Bitcoin transactions occur between electronic Bitcoin wallets, and are digitally signed and verified for security. Thanks to the massive public ledger called the blockchain, users are aware of all transactions. If you send Bitcoin to someone, that transaction will have three pieces of information:

- The amount of Bitcoin
- The recipient's wallet address, generated randomly and consisting of a sequence of letters and numbers – this is where you'll be sending your funds
- A private key, which is also a unique sequence of numbers and letters exclusively available to you. This key will allow you to access your wallet.

Once a transaction is set up, it makes its way into the Bitcoin network where it awaits verification and confirmation. Through the process of mining, miners use software to solve random mathematical problems. Once completed, the transaction successfully moves into the blockchain.

What is the Bitcoin Blockchain?

The blockchain, is a huge, shared public ledger where the entire Bitcoin network is situated. All verified transactions are added to the Blockchain, where everyone can see information pertaining to Bitcoin wallets and verify their balances. Read this article for a nice metaphor of how a blockchain works.

Is Bitcoin Secure?

Bitcoin has a strong track record for security and privacy, thanks to its protocol and cryptography. With private keys, individuals' wallets are kept secure. The only way this would not be true is if users lose this information. Although individual wallets and exchanges have been hacked, the underlying protocol has never been compromised.

Where can I spend Bitcoin?

You can spend them online or in actual stores across a variety of industries –
Check out some of the companies that accept Bitcoin here .

What are Bitcoin Debit Cards?

There are Visa and Mastercard debit cards, so you can spend Bitcoin anywhere Visa or Mastercard is accepted but there may be high transaction fees.

Is Bitcoin Anonymous?

Bitcoin transactions are not tied to any personal information which allows users to protect their privacy. However, since all Bitcoin transactions are public knowledge and permanently on the blockchain, other users can see the activity associated to a particular wallet address—hence not being 100% anonymous. It is highly recommended (to users who want anonymity) to only use Bitcoin addresses once to avoid your identity being revealed either through a specific purchase or other means.

Does Bitcoin have transaction fees?

Normally, Bitcoin transactions have low fees. These fees fluctuate and depend on the dynamic fee market. To speed up your transactions, you can pay a higher fee.

Who controls the Bitcoin network?

Nobody owns the Bitcoin network, much like no one controls the internet. Bitcoin is controlled by all Bitcoin users around the world. While developers are improving the software, they can't force a change in the Bitcoin protocol because all users are free to choose what software and version they use. In order to stay compatible with each other, all users need to use software complying with the same rules. Bitcoin can only work correctly with a complete consensus among all users. Therefore, all users and developers have a strong incentive to protect this consensus. This is one part of what is called "mining". To learn more about Bitcoin, you can consult the dedicated page and the original paper.

Isn't Bitcoin mining a waste of energy?

Some people think so. Like any other payment service, the use of Bitcoin entails processing costs. Services necessary for the operation of currently widespread monetary systems, such as banks, credit cards, and armored vehicles, also use a lot of energy. Although unlike Bitcoin, their total energy consumption is not transparent and cannot be as easily measured.

Bitcoin mining has been designed to become more optimized over time with specialized hardware consuming less energy, and the operating costs of mining should continue to be proportional to demand. When Bitcoin mining becomes too competitive and less profitable, some miners choose to stop their activities. There are other cryptocurrencies which do not use mining. If you are interested in energy free crypto, there are many to choose from.

What do I need to start mining?

In the early days of Bitcoin, anyone could find a new block using their computer's CPU. As more and more people started mining, the difficulty of finding new blocks increased greatly to the point where the only cost-effective method of mining today is using specialized hardware. You can visit **BitcoinMining.com** for more information.

Is Bitcoin really used by people?

Yes. There are a growing number of businesses and individuals using Bitcoin. This includes brick-and-mortar businesses like restaurants, apartments, and law firms, as well as popular online services such as Namecheap, Overstock.com, and Reddit.

While Bitcoin remains a relatively new phenomenon, it is growing fast. At the end of April 2017, the total value of all existing bitcoins exceeded 20 billion US dollars, with millions of dollars worth of bitcoins exchanged daily.

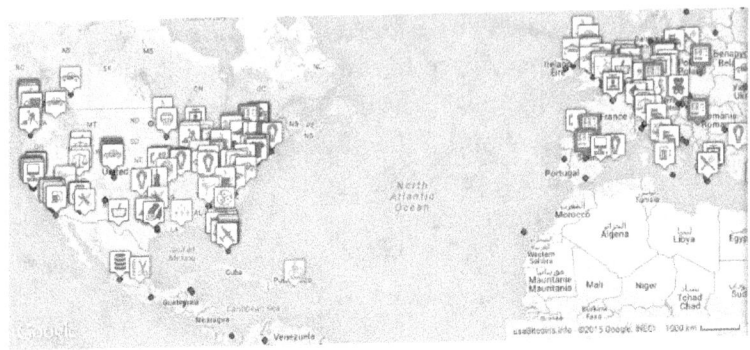

How difficult is it to make a Bitcoin payment?

Bitcoin payments are easier to make than debit or credit card purchases, and can be received without a merchant account. Payments are made from a wallet application,
either on your computer or smartphone, by entering the recipient's address, the payment amount, and pressing send. To make it easier to enter a recipient's address, many wallets can obtain the address by scanning a QR code or touching two phones together with NFC technology.

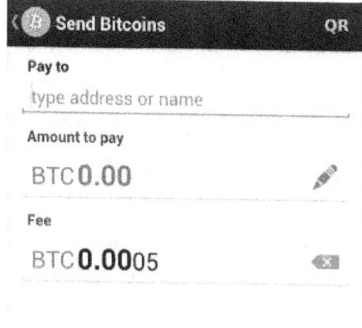

What are the disadvantages of Bitcoin?

- **Degree of acceptance** - Many people are still unaware of Bitcoin. Every day, more businesses accept bitcoins because they want the advantages of doing so, but the list remains small and still needs to grow in order to benefit from network effects .

- **Volatility** - The total value of bitcoins in circulation and the number of businesses using Bitcoin are still very small compared to what they could be.

  Therefore, relatively small events, trades, or business activities can significantly affect the price. In theory, this volatility will decrease as Bitcoin markets and the technology matures. Never before has the world seen a start-up currency, so it is truly difficult (and exciting) to imagine how it will play out.

- **Ongoing development** - Bitcoin software is still in beta with many incomplete features in active development. New tools, features, and services are being developed to make Bitcoin more secure and accessible to the masses. Some of these are still not ready for everyone. Most Bitcoin businesses are new and still offer no insurance. In general, Bitcoin is still in the process of maturing.

Why do people trust Bitcoin?

Much of the trust in Bitcoin comes from the fact that it requires no trust at all. Bitcoin is fully open-source and decentralized. This means that anyone has access to the entire source code at any time. Any developer in the world can therefore verify exactly how Bitcoin works. All transactions and bitcoins issued into existence can be transparently consulted in real-time by anyone. All payments can be made without reliance on a third party and the whole system is protected by heavily peer-reviewed cryptographic algorithms like those used for online banking. No organization or individual can control Bitcoin, and the network remains secure even if not all of its users can be trusted.

Can I make money with Bitcoin?

You should never expect to get rich with Bitcoin or any emerging technology. It is always important to be wary of anything that sounds too good to be true or disobeys basic economic rules.

Bitcoin is a growing space of innovation and there are business opportunities that also include risks. There is no guarantee that Bitcoin will continue to grow even though it has developed at a very fast rate so far. Investing time and resources on anything related to Bitcoin requires entrepreneurship. There are various ways to make money with Bitcoin such as mining, trading or running new businesses.

All of these methods are competitive and there is no guarantee of profit. It is up to each individual to make a proper evaluation of the costs and the risks involved in any such project.

Is Bitcoin digital/virtual/immaterial?

Bitcoin is as virtual as the credit cards and online banking networks people use everyday. Bitcoin can be used to pay online and in physical stores just like any other form of money. paying with a mobile phone usually remains the most convenient way to send and receive bitcoin. Bitcoin balances are stored in a large distributed network, and they cannot be fraudulently altered by anybody. In other words, Bitcoin users have exclusive control over their funds and bitcoins cannot vanish just because they are virtual. Most money in the world such as US Dollars are mostly digital rather than physical. Furthermore, it has not been backed by Gold for a long time.

What happens when bitcoins are lost?

When a user loses access or forgets about their wallet/private key it has the effect of removing the bitcoin from the supply, thus increasing the value of the remaining finite number of bitcoins.

Can Bitcoin scale to become a major payment network?

Perhaps. Bitcoin is always evolving and developing. There are many cryptos which are trying to become competitive with major payment processors. For more details, on bitcoin scaling see this Scalability page.

Is Bitcoin useful for illegal activities?

Yes and so is regular money. This brings a philosophical discussion into play on whether people have the right to privacy from governments.

What about Bitcoin and taxes?

Bitcoin is not a fiat currency with legal tender status in any jurisdiction, but often tax liability accrues regardless of the medium used. There is a wide variety of legislation in many different jurisdictions which could cause income, sales, payroll, capital gains, or some other form of tax liability to arise with Bitcoin.

What about Bitcoin and consumer protection?

Bitcoin does not have the kind of consumer protection that some payment processors are known for. However certain exchanges have insurance for losses much like banks.

Can Bitcoins become worthless?

Yes. It can also rise astronomically. It is not unlike any other currency in this regard.

Isn't speculation and volatility a problem for Bitcoin?

At this time Bitcoin is a volatile asset, but this could change in time. If you would like to use a cryptocurrency with a stable price, see so called stable coins such as DAI and TrueUSD.

What is confirmation?

Receiving notification of a payment is almost instant with Bitcoin. However, there is a delay before the network begins to confirm your transaction by including it in a block.

A confirmation means that there is a consensus on the network that the bitcoins you received haven't been sent to anyone else and are considered your property. Once your transaction has been included in one block, it will continue to be buried under every block after it, which will exponentially consolidate this consensus and decrease the risk of a reversed transaction. Each confirmation takes between a few seconds and 90 minutes, with 10 minutes being the average.

If the transaction pays too low a fee or is otherwise atypical, getting the first confirmation can take much longer. Every user is free to determine at what point they consider a transaction sufficiently confirmed, but 6 confirmations is often considered to be as safe as waiting 6 months on a credit card transaction.

What if I receive Bitcoin when my computer is powered off?

Yes you can accept Bitcoins with your computer/phone off. The bitcoins will appear next time you start your wallet application.

Bitcoins are not actually received by the software on your computer, they are added to a public ledger that is shared between all the devices on the network.

Is Bitcoin vulnerable to quantum computing?

Yes, most systems relying on cryptography in general are, including traditional banking systems. However, quantum computers don't yet exist and probably won't for a while. In the event that quantum computing could be an imminent threat to Bitcoin, the protocol could be upgraded to use post-quantum algorithms. Given the importance that this update would have, it can be safely expected that it would be highly reviewed by developers and adopted by all Bitcoin users.

When buying a Bitcoin, do you have to buy a whole one?

No, you can buy a ½, a ¼, a 1/10, all the way to the hundredth millionth place, etc.
Many beginners think that Bitcoin is expensive, but don't recognize that most people only buy fractions of a Bitcoin. Remember that the price of a coin does not determine its underlying value.

END OF BITCOIN SPECIFIC SECTION

What is a crypto/cryptocurrency?

Cryptocurrency is virtual currency, an exchange medium that uses cryptography in order to control the creation of the system units and secure its transactions. Bitcoin was the first and remains the biggest crypto.

What is the difference between a "Coin" and a "Token" ?

A Coin is a cryptocurrency that operates independently.
A Token is a cryptocurrency that depends on another cryptocurrency as a platform to operate. Check out the crypto tokens listings to view a list of tokens and their respective platforms.

What is an AltCoin?

An AltCoin is an Alternative Coin. All cryptos other than Bitcoin are considered AltCoins.

Do Exchanges Need My Personal Documents?

In order to buy or sell cryptos, many sites require you to identify yourself using a government ID. This may not be the case with peer to peer services.

Can you transfer Cryptocurrency between countries?

Yes! Cryptocurrency is a decentralized payment system in which it allows its user to exchange without the involvement of a financial institution. It has a superb authentication system and unique design to send payment at almost instant at the lowest cost anywhere in the world. Crypto is not limited by borders!

How many cryptocurrencies exist?

The number of cryptocurrencies grows every day. They are divided into two groups: Bitcoin (that stands alone in one group) or Altcoins (all other cryptocurrencies). This is because the code of cryptocurrency is open source , this means that anyone has the chance to create their own version of cryptocurrency by just adapting the code. Check CoinYou.Co/Prices for a nice list of cryptos with real-time prices and additional information.

What was the first cryptocurrency?

The first cryptocurrency was Bitcoin, created in 2009.

What are the most common cryptocurrencies?

1. Bitcoin : This cryptocurrency was the first in the ecosystem and the most commonly traded cryptocurrency today. In 2009 Satoshi Nakamoto developed Bitcoin, an anonymous person or group of persons.

2. Ethereum : 2015 is the year Ethereum was born, a token based currency used in Ethereum blockchain, it is placed in the second in rank on the most valuable and popular cryptocurrency in the marketplace. Ethereum has smart contracts. See smart contracts definition below.

3. Ripple : A cryptocurrency for interbank transfers created in 2012. Ripple has a feature to track the type of transaction made, not just cryptocurrency.
Ripple has been used by UBS and Santander.

4. Litecoin : Litecoin is a cryptocurrency that is similar to bitcoin, but moves quickly on its developments, this includes faster payments and processes more transactions at a time.

See a list at coinyou.co/prices

How is cryptocurrency value determined?

The value is determined by the going rate on exchanges, whatever parties agree to pay each other. This means, there is no fixed price, price changes are based on supply and demand.

What are the worst things about crypto?

The worst thing about crypto, or the worst for the the beginners, is the complexity of the matter in the first place. It takes some time for people who don't know much about computation and the financial system/economics to start to appreciate the solutions that Bitcoin and Altcoins create. Some other potentially complicated things in this field relate to regulatory uncertainty and the technical problems in scaling the crypto systems in order for them to compete with current payment methods such as debit/credit cards. There are many challenges with cryptocurrencies, they are an emerging technology.

Is cryptocurrency Legal?

Check this link to check the laws related to Bitcoin in your country: https://en.wikipedia.org/wiki/Legality_of_bitcoin_by_country_or_territory

Is cryptocurrency safe?

It is important to do your due diligence to research the stability and security of the tokens, wallets, and exchanges you use. In some ways cryptocurrency offers more security than regular money but in other ways it offers less protection. It is more secure because a bank or government cannot confiscate it. It has less protection because it has no fraud protection.

One central safety issue is that you are responsible for the security of the funds in your possession, one does that by following best practices regarding security. See security course on https://CoinYou.co

What are the benefits of cryptocurrency?

Learn more about the benefits of low transaction fees, anonymity, and control/freedom in the following article/video: Click Here.

What is the difference between cryptocurrency and digital currency? Are they both the same?

Most currencies in the world exist as digital currency (numbers in bank accounts for example). Only a small percentage exist as physical cash. Cryptocurrency is also in a digital format, however it is not usually controlled by central authorities. An additional feature of crypto is that it uses cryptography to ensure security.

CRYPTO GLOSSARY

What is a cryptocurrency exchange and market?

A cryptocurrency market and exchange are both services on the web, allowing cryptocurrency token holders to trade to other currencies. CoinYou recommends CEX.io , Changelly and Binance .

What is " Market Capitalization " and how is it calculated?

Market Capitalization is one way to rank the relative size of a cryptocurrency. It's calculated by multiplying the Price by the Circulating Supply . Price X Circulating Supply. The total worth of all coins in circulation for a particular crypto.

What is the difference between "Circulating Supply", "Total Supply", and "Max Supply" ?

Circulating Supply is the best approximation of the number of coins that are circulating in the market and in the general public's hands. Total Supply is the total amount of coins in existence right now (minus any coins that have been verifiably burned).

Max Supply is the best approximation of the maximum amount of coins that will ever exist in the lifetime of the cryptocurrency.

What is FUD?

FUD stands for Fear, Uncertainty, and Doubt. Whether it is based on legitimate concerns and is justified, or due to a lack of information or unreliable news made public with the calculated intent to harm the marlek. Often, when people that could be contributors or investors in cryptos have doubts, it is due to FUD.

What is FOMO?

FOMO stands for Fear of Missing Out. When people are afraid that they will lose a chance to invest in a project before the price goes up, it is called FOMO. Ironically, when many people invest in a project due to this phenomenon, the price can go up and can cause a bubble that crashes causing the value of the investment to go down.

What does HODL mean?

HODL has been said to stand for Hold On For Dear Life. It generally means to hold onto a crypto investment for long term gains. You can learn about the origin here: https://en.wikipedia.org/wiki/Hodl

What is a whale?

A whale is an investor with millions or billions of dollars worth of crypto, who is capable of manipulating market prices.

What does pump and dump mean?

To pump a crypto is to increase it's market value. To dump a crypto is to sell it. Some market manipulators cause a crypto to increase in value in order to sell for gains and then buy back at a lower price, repeating the cycle many times.

What is shilling?

Shilling is promoting a crypto, sometimes using false promises or lies.

What is a shill?

A shill is a person who promotes a crypto, sometimes when they are paid to do so.

What does "moon" and "lambo" mean?

To moon is a verb which means a crypto price goes high like the moon. A lambo is often mentioned in crypto forums referring to the trend of instant crypto millionaires who buy lamborghinis.

What does DLT stand for?

DLT stands for Distributed Ledger Technology such as blockchain. A ledger is just an accounting of information. Distributed means it is stored in various places rather than in a central place.

What is a node?

Any computer or computing device that connects to a network is called a node.

What does decentralized mean?

Central means one place. Decentralized means more than one point or node is used to store information for example. Distributed also means decentralized.

What is a sh*t coin?

A shit coin is a coin that should not have monetary value because it does not provide any other kind of value to anyone.

What does token utility mean?

This refers to whether or not a token serves a purpose other than speculation.

What is a security?

A security is like a public stock, it is a regulated monetary instrument intended for investment profit.

What is a telegram or discord channel?

These are social media apps, often used for crypto information sharing.

What are trading signals?

Trading signals are timed investment advice for trading crypto.

What is BitConnect?

BitConnect is a pyramid scheme scam that stole many peoples' money with the promise of making them more money.

What is Tether?

Tether is a crypto pegged to the USD. Exchanges use it instead of the USD to avoid regulation. It is unclear if

Tether is actually a scam. New stable coins, which are more transparent are being created.

What is Google Authenticator?

Google Authenticator is an app used for security purposes for crypto wallets.

What is an ERC20 Token?

An ERC20 token is the most popular token for crypto projects to launch their own currency on the Ethereum Blockchain. Metamask is a wallet for storing ERC20 Tokens.

What is an ICO?

ICO stands for Initial Coin Offering. Similar to a public stock Initial Public Offering, it is for projects to raise money by selling tokens in exchange for money or crypto.

What is a fork?

Blockchains can create a copy of the protocol for various reasons such as creating similar cryptos or avoiding problems from past errors. Expand

What does DOS attack mean?

A DOS or Denial of Service attack is when hackers blast a website with visits to cause problems or steal money.

What does remittance mean?

A remittance is a payment, usually it refers to a cross-border payment.

What is Github?

Github is a site for tech projects to store open or closed source code to share with their team or the tech community.

What does immutable mean?

Immutable means you cannot change it...ever. You cannot change the records of Bitcoin transactions. They are stored permanently and cannot be altered.

What does protocol mean?

When computers communicate with each other, there needs to be a common set of rules and instructions that each computer follows. A specific set of communication rules is called a protocol.

What does trustless mean?

When you do not have to rely on trust, it is trustless. With DLT or blockchain transactions, you do not have to rely or trust a central authority to verify or store information.

What is Inflation?

A general increase in prices and fall in the purchasing value of money. When governments/central banks increase the money supply, it can cause the value of the money to fall.

What is fiat?

Any money declared by a government to be legal tender. (valid money) US Dollars are Fiat currency.

Does Bitcoin have inflation?

Not after it meets the maximum supply of 21 million coins.

What is crypto mining?

Since the economics differ from each coin it's best to look at this generally speaking.

Mining is a means to verify transactions done on a decentralized network and introduce new coins into the ecosystem. With mining, a miner has a cost of electricity they have to spend to solve a "mathematical problem" that is checked by other participants in the network to see if it's correct or not. If it's found to be incorrect the work that miner has done is eventually considered invalid and they are given no reward for their work, if it's found to be valid they are rewarded with newly minted coins and some of the transaction fees from the network.

What is a smart contract?

A smart contract is a programmable agreement between parties that will execute as expected without one needing to worry about outside influence.

What is a (smart) contract address?

When a blockchain developer sets up a smart contract she can also connect an address to this contract. This is called a contract address. These kinds of addresses are different from a wallet address. It is important to understand this when you contribute to initial coin offerings on Ethereum, Neo, or other smart contract blockchains.

What is the difference between cold storage and hot storage?

Cold storage refers to storage that is disconnected from the internet. Hot storage is a piece of hardware (smartphone, computers) that is connected to the Internet.

What are Public and Private Keys?

Cryptocurrency is represented by an entry in the blockchain associated to a public key, it's kind of like your account number or your address.

In order to move currency around, exchange it, make a purchase with it, or convert it back to FIAT money, your private key is required to unlock it. Typically, your private key is stored within your wallet, or online. Its like your password or the key to your safe. If you lose your private key, your cryptocurrency is lost. Similar to losing the key to an impenetrable safe. This is why it is very important to consider how your private keys are stored.

What is a seed phrase?

A seed phrase is a private key that is a series of random words to restore and control your crypto account. You should not save it or share it to a device connected to the internet.

What is a Multisig Wallet?

A multisig cryptocurrency wallet, also known as a "multi-signature" wallet, refers to a cryptocurrency wallets types that require input from multiple parties in order to complete a transaction. Consider types of cryptocurrency wallet that use multisig technology like a shared bank account, here all parties need to enter their PIN or order to complete a transaction.

What is a Multi-Currency Wallet?

Some wallets only hold one type of cryptocurrency, Multi-Currency wallets allow you to store multiple types of cryptocurrencies.

What is an Online Wallet? (Web Wallet)?

Online Wallets are cryptocurrency wallets that can be used with a web browser like Google Chrome or Firefox.

What is a Mobile Wallet?

Mobile wallets usually can be used with mobile devices. Therefore they provide additional features in comparison with completely internet-based wallets, but they also have additional security risks.

What is a Desktop Wallet?

A desktop wallet is usually a software program on the computer where cryptocurrencies are stored. They are considered more secure than online and mobile wallets, but that also depends on the user's commitment to security.

What is a hardware wallet?

A hardware wallet is a device with which the user can store cryptocurrencies disconnected from the internet. This is one of the most secure ways to store crypto.

CoinYou recommends Trezor brand wallets. Learn more in our security courses.

What is a paper wallet?

A paper wallet is a wallet, where the private and public key is printed together on a paper, disconnected from the internet. Examples: BitAddress.org and Bitcoin Armory can help you create and print your paper wallet.

CoinYou's mission is to onboard people into the crypto ecosystem. Most people have no idea what crypto is and how it works. Crypto knowledge is mostly held by young, wealthy, English speaking men in the developed world. CoinYou intends to train the other 99 percent, such as the unbanked and refugees, but also corporate employees in a multilingual app with moderated social forums.
Anyone can translate or submit content, but it must meet our guidelines...education without speculation.

No "get rich quick" schemes. We are a trusted gateway into the crypto world and make crypto's intimidating complexity seem easy and user friendly. Join the CoinYou community for free and download our free apps for Android and iOS. Learn from our mentors in the family friendly social forums and take free 3 minute courses about crypto. Learn how to buy, save, send, spend, and sell crypto safely at CoinYou.Co .

Join Our Communities @CoinYou

Contact Us

All inquiries including press and how to become an instructor, partner, vendor, and advertiser, use contact@coinyou.co

www.ingramcontent.com/pod-product-compliance
Lightning Source LLC
Chambersburg PA
CBHW030043230526
45472CB00005B/1646